She Held A Gun To My Head

Elizabeth Ann Oates
&
Sarah Jane Oates

chipmunkapublishing
the mental health publisher

Published by

Chipmunkapublishing

PO Box 6872

Brentwood

Essex CM13 1ZT

United Kingdom

http://www.chipmunkapublishing.com

Copyright © Elizabeth Ann Oates & Sarah Jane Oates 2012

Edited by Clare Younger

ISBN   978-1-84991-854-1

Chipmunkapublishing   gratefully   acknowledge   the support of Arts Council England.

Elizabeth Oates & Sarah Jane Oates

This book is written for Mam and Dad, Sal and Michael.

With love x

She Held A Gun To My Head

Acknowledgements

Sarah:

I would like to thank Elizabeth, Mam and Dad, Sal and Michael. Without the covert support from my family I sincerely believe I would not have survived. What I mean by covert is not so much direct support, but how they were there for me, they would listen, but they wouldn't push me away and they didn't abandon me. Not once did anyone come up to me and say: "You've got anorexia. Do something about it!"

So the support was fantastic because there was no pressure; there was never any shouting or upset. In hindsight, I think they knew the best thing for me was time - to sort it out in my own mind.

With this in mind, words cannot describe how I would like to thank you all.

To all those who put up with me during those fourteen years, I can't even begin to say how sorry I am. You knew a Sarah who didn't exist - false. It was a lie; it wasn't me.

Dr Claire Weekes, author of the book *Self Help for Your Nerves*

Liz Hill, Specialist Practitioner in Eating Disorders

Dr Moon, GP in Richmond

Jen Cotton, CBT Therapist, Tees, Esk & Wear Valley NHS Trust

Dr Gayer, North House Surgery, Crook

Rachel Donnington, OCD Therapist, Talking Changes, Willington Surgery

Elizabeth:

I would like to thank Sarah for writing this book with me ☺

About the Book

This book is a true story about a set of twins. One had, and is now recovering from, anorexia and the other one thought she was going to lose her. It is a book about sadness, happiness, signs and symptoms of anorexia and how it affects friends and family.

The book is laid out in interview style, with Elizabeth and Sarah chatting, discussing and debating about anorexia. Elizabeth asks Sarah questions and Sarah asks Elizabeth questions.

The book is designed to be cathartic, and to help others who are suffering from anorexia, or who know of someone suffering from anorexia.

Elizabeth and Sarah have always vowed to live to reach their 100th birthday; anything over that is a bonus. Sarah developed anorexia at sixteen and admitted she had it at 30. Elizabeth told Sarah at 28 that while she still had the anorexia she could not see her anymore, even if they did reach their 100th birthday.

Elizabeth decided she had to let Sarah go - it was too painful even to see her, to be in the same room. She would rather have not seen Sarah at all; Sarah was dead to her. Sarah even told Elizabeth that she felt dead.

This book has been written by the twins at age 32. They both felt that the fact Sarah had admitted her problem, and was seeking help and getting better, was cause for celebration for themselves and their family. They both wanted to write this book as a celebration and to help others.

They plan to live life as much as they can, for they appreciate how short it can be.

Contents

She Held A Gun To My Head

Part 1:

Introducing Elizabeth and Sarah and the reason for the book

E:

Hi readers, my name's Elizabeth Oates, and I'm 32. I am known to my twin as Pea. I was born and live in County Durham, England. I have short hair and class myself as a tomboy. Sarah is the one with the eyelash curlers and is always faffing with her hair!

S:

Hello, my name's Sarah Jane Oates and yes, I speak as the recovering anorexic. I am also known to my twin as Pea (peas in a pod). I am proud of who I am, what I was and who I aim to become. I think anorexia is a deadly disease of the mind which can only be treated by the mind. If you don't have the right mind you are dead, it kills you. If you aren't strong enough it eats the mind. Before we start the interview I would like to warn the readers that there is raw emotion in this book. I do not intend to hold back any feelings that I have had or have now.

But I DO NOT intend to hurt or upset any readers.

E:

I want to write this book as a celebration to Sarah - well, to us really. She has had, and is now recovering from, anorexia and I always believed she wouldn't make it past 30. That is what I'd heard you see: most anorexics don't make it past 30. When we got to 28 and Sarah was still anorexic, I gave up on her, and myself really. I couldn't live with seeing her like that anymore, so I didn't want to see her anymore. This ate me up and I ended up in hospital, in a mental ward. Afterwards I told Sarah just how much it had affected me, and this was her wake up call.

Now I want to publish this book as a celebration to Sarah, and to myself. And to all other anorexics and families out there who suffer. Anorexia is a HORRIBLE,

HORRIBLE thing and I say to those who have had it (and their families): you are an inspiration.

Let me describe Sarah. You are the wild one, the one who breaks the rules, the one who says things perhaps others wouldn't at a party. You are funny, and thoughtful towards me. You are flighty, lively. You look like Bambi when you run – in a cute way! You are beautiful when you really smile, and when you laugh, and when you have some weight on – around your face and your legs. You always make sure your bed is cosy on a night. If I ever want something, you'll have it there for me instantly. I remember one time when we were out shopping, I said I needed a pen. Then you said, "Right, I'll get you a pen!" You dived into the betting shop we were passing and shot back out with a little pen. I couldn't believe it; you always delivered. You'd make a fantastic PA!

I learn things from you. I learn that boundaries CAN be pushed and that we should not live so restrictively.

Oh and there was this other time, I wanted some money when we were in the pub, and you threw a penny straight across the bar and onto the bar opposite us. It was a busy bar but you didn't hit a soul! I couldn't believe it - I cringed! You'd also throw beer mats around the place, and no-one would bat an eyelid. How do you do that?

I know how you'd describe me!...A little cute fluffy rabbit, who always found the cutest friends and lived in a cute forest, eating cakes and knitting teddy bears.

S:

Now let me describe you. You are happy, sunny, always see the good in people, fluffy, light, floaty BUT NOT dizzy. On a dull day there's still sunshine - you make even the horrible-est, nastiest things so nice! Full of life, you don't care what you look like but you have great self-respect (whereas I don't really give a crap). I admire you for that.

E:

How do you feel about writing this book with me?

S:

Highly excited! I even thought about the idea myself!

E:

Why do you want to write the book? What do you want to achieve?

S:

To increase awareness of anorexia. And how deadly it is!! People these days don't understand the SERIOUSNESS of all these skinny images and low fat foods. I think it is disgraceful the way agencies use skinny models and that global advertising is still allowed to use such images. THEY SHOULD BE BANNED. Seemingly perfect bodily images should not be used to sell things and make people feel better. I think some of the advertising campaigns are a load of tosh.

I want to make everyone aware of how serious anorexia is...I think people need to more aware of it...oh no, I keep saying the same thing!

E:

But what do you want to achieve?

S:

That's it...I want to increase awareness. It is a disease. People don't understand how a mental illness can kill, just like a physical disease can.

I'm still annoyed about seeing all these skinny models and about the way celebrities are always celebrating how much weight they've lost, and how positive it all is.

E:

Can I just interrupt?...

...But weight loss is good when the person actually wants to lose it to feel better about themselves.

S:

I guess, but they must stop at their natural body weight.

E:

Yes I agree too.

S:

But if we didn't have all these images and lived in the middle of a desert, without all this media saturation, all these unhealthy images, then we wouldn't feel pressured to look at certain way and to fit in. And look beautiful.

E:

Yes, I think being beautiful comes from the inside, from the person, and how happy they are.

S:

I strongly agree. I JUST WANT EVERYONE TO KNOW...

...GETTING OBSESSED WITH WEIGHT CAN KILL YOU, because the mind is a fragile thing and once it has certain thought processes, it's very difficult to go back. I can honestly say this as someone who's had anorexia.

E:

The thoughts go down a negative spiral.

S:

Yep.

E:

Now let's move on to the next chapter: When it all started.

She Held A Gun To My Head

Part 2

When it all started

E:

It all started when we went to sixth form college. Sarah, what do you remember?

S:

A tiny marmalade sandwich with no butter (Weight Watchers bread) at nine a.m. as I was so hungry. So this was lunch and breakfast.

E:

I'm confused, what did you have to eat?

S:

No breakfast, the marmalade sandwich at nine a.m. which was supposed to be my lunch, then chewing gum to keep me going for the rest of the day until teatime.

E:

What time was teatime?

S:

About 7 - Mam made it. And then I remember going to bed absolutely starving. But I got used to it and it was nice. It really affected my sleep but I woke up feeling great, as my stomach was empty.

E:

I remember you appeared to be having fun, and not to have a care in the world. It seemed like a nice life. You missed some lessons.

S:

Ahhhhh...that was because I was high. I was so hungry I was high. And at this point I was having fun because I was getting thinner and thinner. Did I miss some lessons? Where was I?

E:

Well, I remember our Geography teacher asking where you were. And I said you were in bed. You didn't have the energy to get up.

S:

That's horrible! I don't even remember that.

E:

I remember one thing that sticks out in my mind - Mam trying to give you a slice of toast after sixth form, and you refusing and refusing to eat it. There was no shouting or door slamming, just the toast left there on your desk. Not very nice.

When we were at sixth form, I developed bulimia. I remember I threw an Easter egg in the bin outside in the courtyard, because I knew I would eat all of it and then feel so guilty. I remember the guilt - it ate me up and I felt SO angry, SO guilty.

I remember sitting on my bedroom floor after dinner one evening, drinking and drinking a 1.5 litre bottle of Evian so I could be sick. I would use the shower room downstairs which was in the granny flat, so Mam and Dad couldn't hear. I'm not sure if they did; they could have, but I'm too embarrassed to ask even now.

S:

What else can you remember from when we were at sixth form?

E:

As a family we were always discussing you and the anorexia. It made me frustrated as I felt like we were just going around in circles, every month the same conversation! "She's losing weight again, she's flitting from here to there, she only buys pieces of fruit and veg and tiny other things for her weekly shop." "She runs all the time! She has a bowl of fruit after running ten miles!"

It went on and on. I so wanted to help you. You'd say to me you were better, but then the signs were still there. We'd still have the same conversations though.

She Held A Gun To My Head

Part 3

Leaving Home and off to university/travelling

E:

I chose a university in Bristol because I liked the course, the uni itself and the city.

S:

Long way though!

E:

282 miles to be exact. Yeah I know. I liked the idea that it was far. Strange as I found the first few months really hard. I must have been homesick as I used to cry and come all the way home on a weekend. Once I travelled at about midnight and made it home in three hours. I was going through some roadworks on the motorway and remember the moon flashing through the trees.

S:

But it was the speed camera flashing at you!

E:

Yeah, yeah I know! What a story.

Pause

S:

So why did you choose to go all the way down south when you found it so hard to be away?

E:

Looking back, I think I deserved the homesickness - to go through it, to prove to myself that I could do it. Strange. I think I wanted to have a life by myself, not as a twin.

I remember for a few years I didn't like being a twin. I wanted to make my own circle of friends. I did and I loved it. You came to visit me for a couple of weeks and you loved it. You befriended my friends and I loved having you, but I also hated the fact that you were taking my friends.

It's petty but true, and strange how it affected me!

S:

And then you went to Holland.

E:

Yeah, I exchanged in The Netherlands with the uni and I absolutely LOVED it. I could move there!

S:

It was good.

E:

Yeah, you visited me there too for a couple of weeks.

S:

And then Camp USA?

E:

Uh-huh. You came out there too! What a pattern eh Pea?

S:

But I never came to Australia.

E:

Oh no! Was I that bad? Did I want to get away so much that I went to Australia? I think that has just clicked, opps.

S:

Yeah, Australia? A little far for little me to travel.

E:

Anyway I adored all my travelling, and would do it again and again, to different places. Every now and again I would tell you to try Camp USA or something like that, but you always said you weren't strong enough. I thought you were, and that was what you needed, but I don't think you could see yourself doing it so didn't believe in yourself.

S:

Remember that while you were in Bristol, I was at Leeds Uni?

E:

Yeah, doing Fine Art. And you found it so difficult you transferred back home to Newcastle Uni for your last year.

S:

Leeds was fun but hard. You came up a few times.

E:

I had fun at your digs and I thought your art studio space was amazing. It was so white!

S:

You remember that?

E:

Of course! Remember the washing machine you taped up?

S:

Ha! Yes! I found it on a road, wheeled it in, and taped it up with yellow and green striped insulation tape.

E:

I thought you were mad, and loved it – a true fine artist. Thing is, you were a little mad, and poorly.

S:

Yeah. Leeds was cold. So I went back home.

E:

Hey, but you were worse BEFORE you went to university. Remember? At Newcastle COLLEGE?

S:

Yes, where I did my foundation arts course.

E:

That was horrible. Possibly the worst I've seen you. I think of it now and I could cry. You were there in your little digs – a nice room in that block overlooking the river. But you struggled, and you hated it, I knew. I had to leave you there though. I wanted you to get stronger, and myself too for when I saw you.

You know I can't remember much from back then. Can you?

S:

Yes. I was tired. I didn't spend much time at college as I didn't have any energy. It was down the hill from my flat.

E:

And you had to walk back up the hill to get home?

S:

Yes. It's not a big hill but seemed big at the time. I went to the gym a lot and ran a lot.

E:

Around the town?

S:

No around the rough areas.

E:

Did you make friends with your flatmates?

S:

Yes, I suppose. I went out to the pub with them but just remember getting drunk a lot.

I had the dark red bob - extreme hairdo.

E:

Yes, I remember that.

Elizabeth Oates & Sarah Jane Oates

Part 4

Full-blown Anorexia

E:

Tell me Sarah, how long would you say you had anorexia?

S:

Fourteen years.

E:

So am I right in saying that it got worse?

S:

Yep. After years of abuse, starvation, self neglect and self harm (depriving myself of nutrition), it eventually took its toll on my body.

E:

How do you mean?

S:

Teeth.

E:

No, I mean before that. I saw things before your teeth were damaged.

S:

Okay then. My hair was very thin and straw-like. So I had it cut short in a bob and I dyed it. My skin lost all its colour. I was very pale.

E:

I noticed you had sunken eyes, and I'm sure you said you had no chin.

S:

Also I was told I had downy hair.

E:

I've heard about this. I've got longer hair on my arms.

S:

No, it's different. It's the body's way of keeping itself warm and it's very prominent on anorexics, particularly on the face. It's a protective mechanism built into the body to help keep a person warm during periods of malnutrition. Its medical name is lanugo (source: Sheffield Eating Disorders Service, Sheffield Care Trust, NHS).

E:

Yes I know. In the winter, when you were outside, I

could see it on your face.   It was quite cute but also worrying.

S:

Now my teeth are permanently damaged.   All the enamel has gone across the gum lines and you can see this when I smile. It's really affected my confidence.

E:

But you do smile a lot and I don't think it's a big issue for you. This is fantastic and you should keep it up.

S:

There are some foods that make my teeth hurt but I still do eat them.

E:

Why?

S:

'Cos I enjoy them.

E:

So let's talk more about the physical effects on the body.

S:

Well now...my circulation still isn't normal.

E:

How was it during the anorexia?

S:

Painful to say the least. The only time I felt warm was in a hot bath. As soon as I got out the bath, I was cold again. The word cold doesn't describe how cold it was for me. It was a chilling cold, right to the bone. But now I don't feel that, so in a way my circulation is much improved, but I do still feel cold when it's actually quite warm. I still wear jumpers in the summer and always have to have one with me.

E:

Right, so tell about the mental effects of the anorexia.

S:

Okay...I could not be in company at meal times. And this got so bad, I isolated myself from everybody. So I just didn't spend any time with anybody at all.

E:

What did anorexia do to you then? How did it affect your lifestyle?

S:

Well...I lost quite a few good relationships. I could not hold down a job because I couldn't concentrate and my days were based around food. Also, I was too cold and couldn't fit into the uniforms! I couldn't even wear black trousers!

I had to transfer universities to be close to my hometown where I knew my family were.

When I did have a job, I remember drinking energy drinks to keep me going to finish the shift.

E:

Did you not use toothpaste as I've heard anorexics don't because it's calorific?

S:

What?!! I've never heard of that one! But I do remember looking forward to brushing my teeth because it felt like I was eating.

E:

Did you also smell food and pretend you were eating it? Like almost eating the smell?

S:

Oh yes. It's a trick. You trick the mind to believe it is eating so it's like you really are eating.

E:

ALSO cooking for people - a big anorexic trait?

S:

Again... yes. I used to cook big family dinners and pretend I had already eaten.

E:

AND smell the cooking?

S:

Yes.

E:

SO that's why you took a job in a restaurant?

S:

Yes. I actually believed I enjoyed this work...the catering industry. I enjoyed cooking for people, and preparing and being around the food.

E:

What about drinking?

S:

Water - that's all I could drink. That's all I was allowed to drink.

E:

Allowed? I know...the anorexic talking?

S:

Indeed, the anorexic only allowed me to drink water.

E:

Here's another one...what about foods that you can trick people with...with the cucumber?

S:

What?!

E:

Well it's mostly water yes?

S:

Oh yes I get it now. Yes I did that as well.

E:

I've heard you mention the traffic light system recently. What is this? Is this your own technique?

S:

No, no. It's a theory that my therapist told me about and said I was doing it.

E:

So what is it, in a sentence?

S:

Basically green foods are safe, orange foods are okay and red represents DANGER foods.

E:

Well actually, I thought you were doing that all those years! I used to think you put foods in categories like that.   Like the cucumber is good!   But cheese is BAD!!!!!!

S:

Yes that's it!

E:

Tell me more!

S:

Bad foods: onions, beetroot, CHEESE, crisps, mayonnaise, white bread, pasta, fizzy drinks.

Okay foods: brown bread.

Safe foods: apples, cucumbers - any fruit or veg.

E:

Hold on...you said some veg was bad?

S:

Oh yes, that's confusing. I guess to me all fruit was good/safe, but only some veg was good.

E:

You used to eat A LOT of cereal, even having it as a main meal in the evening. Why was this?

S:

Simple...I could skip the main meal, pretend I was eating breakfast and then skip breakfast altogether the next day.

E:

So what about signs? Are there any more traits?

S:

Yes. Using a small fork or small teaspoon to eat with. Also a small plate. Soup and water to fill me up. Apples would also fill me up.

E:

When I had bulimia I used to chew gum to burn energy. Did you do this?

S:

No, I didn't know that was true.

I only ate at certain times of the day.

E:

Also, when I had bulimia I would only eat at night. I'd wait all day to prove to myself that I could do it, then pig out at night.

S:

Yes I did that too sometimes, especially when went out as a family. I would eat all the desserts and have seconds, as I thought it wasn't proper food. Then afterwards I would feel so sick, and so guilty, but to make myself feel better I'd eat more.

E:

I did the same. You also had a fertility test at the hospital to see if you could conceive?

S:

Yep.

E:

Didn't your periods stop altogether, and this was why you had the test?

S:

Yes. After several years without periods, I became increasingly worried about my future and being able to have children, which was (and still is) something I definitely wish to do.

E:

What was the test result?

S:

To my astonishment, everything was honky-doodle. So I am very much looking forward to having children in the future.

However, at that point I was still in denial.

E:

What, when you had the test?

S:

Yes. I was still in denial. I continued to starve myself, not even thinking about it. Very odd now when I look back. It is very, very serious and this is what anorexia can do. It changes the way you think and what you think about. You forget about the most important things in life.

E:

Quite.

She Held A Gun To My Head

Part 5

Sarah denied access into hospital for treatment

E:

I remember coming to see you one night. I sat you down and told you I thought it was a good idea for you to go into hospital. I told you that we couldn't help you anymore and that I thought you needed proper full time supervision. I felt such a weight off when I said this to you. I didn't want to put words in your mouth or force you to go in, and was so happy when you agreed with me. You put the wheels in motion straight away.

S:

Yes, but they wouldn't let me go in. They said I wasn't bonkers and my BMI wasn't low enough.

E:

This makes me so angry - that someone like you wants help but because you're not on the floor going mad or dying, they turn you away.

S:

I wanted to go into hospital but because I couldn't go in, I made my own rehab by purposely isolating myself from the world so I could recover.

E:

This is amazing Sarah. I'm proud of you for this!

S:

At this point I knew I had to do this on my own. NO-ONE and NOTHING could help. I remember when I went shopping, I just bought the basic stuff and wore the same clothes. I couldn't watch television or listen to music. I COULD NOT LISTEN TO ANY MUSIC – IT WAS HORRENDOUS. Life was too much to bear. I couldn't decide on anything. I spent a good few months doing nothing. I would sit and stare at nothing. My mind was a mush. I could hardly open my eyes. But I wasn't tired. I don't want to say I was reborn, just wide awake, enlightened if you like, but so utterly exhausted.

It was the hardest time of my life. I think THIS WAS HARDER THAN THE ANOREXIA. I think it was the shock and the fact that I'd isolated myself so I couldn't go out. I was utterly paranoid because I now knew that when people looked at me, they were looking at an anorexic. I was utterly embarrassed and ashamed. I knew now that I had to get better but until I did, I couldn't face the world.

E:

Do you think you still had anorexia then?

S:

Yes. Even though I wanted to go into hospital, it wasn't like the wake-up call that was coming.

E:

Yeah. You still seemed to be sucked into the anorexia somehow.

S:

I did keep a journal during this stage of my life. I lived alone about an hour from home. I moved there to get away - I realise this now. Here are some extracts from my journal...

E:

I didn't know you kept a journal then. I suppose I wouldn't, as we didn't see much of each other at that time.

S:

Monday...

"Something was wrong. Extremely wrong. Everything was blurry. I went to work as normal. But I had lost all concentration . What was happening? Why did everything feel wrong?

I felt like I was going to explode.

The following day...

Off sick. I couldn't breathe properly. I thought I was having a very slow heart attack. Made an urgent doctor's appointment. She signed me off sick for the foreseeable future.

That week…

I stayed indoors and cried. Cried. Couldn't speak, just cried. Stared into nothing. I walked. I sat. And I cried.

The worst week of my life?

Yes.

The following week…

Had another doctor's appointment.   My sister-in-law drove for over an hour to come with me. Thank you Claire. I couldn't stop crying. I thought I was in a far away hole. A deep dark hole that I couldn't get out of.

This was the worst day of my life.

My doctor (Dr. Moon), asked me lots of questions. Claire sat with me for support.

Of the words that I could say, I managed to tell her that I needed help.

Desperate, urgent help. Now.

I can still feel the emotion. As I write this I can feel it deep down. I can feel the sadness and the desperate plea for help.

"This I could not tackle on my own.

This was way out of my league.

Today I admitted I had anorexia.

Sincerely, the darned hardest thing I have ever, ever done.

And by God, of anything I have faced or may have to face in the future, I can assure you nothing was or will be as hard and painful as this."

E:

That's quite a strong thing to say.

S:

During the next several months...

"Friday...

Had toast for breakfast. Excellent progress! Felt panicky all day. Couldn't get the horrid toast out of my head. Nasty food. Felt ugly.

Must keep eating.

Saturday...

My body hurts. Feel heavy. So bloated.

Sunday...

Suicidal thoughts.

Car...

Speed…

Shit."

E:

I sure know that feeling. It's horrid.

S:

The following Friday…

"Suicidal. Accepting thought. Allowing myself to float with it. Teaching myself to accept bad thought.

Not good, but have no energy to worry about it.

Forget about your past you idiot. Accept it and move on. You can do it.

Think you are a character in your own life movie. Be that character who you want to be. Go where she is. Wear what she is wearing. Speak how she speaks.

Feel good?

Well make that person you. Be that character.

Sunday…

MUST TELL DOCTOR! I am still having suicidal thoughts!

I am so tired of eating!

I haven't gained any weight!

Monday…

Went to butchers to buy a fresh steak. Cooked it just how I like. Beautiful.

An hour later ate a whole packet of biscuits with butter and jam on each biscuit (????)…then a chocolate muffin…

Oh my…I felt disgusting…

Words cannot describe how pathetic, weak and useless I felt that night."

E:

I can appreciate how you felt. It felt the same with my bulimia. The guilt just takes over.

S:

"Thoughts of speeding car were flashing through my mind…

I went to bed utterly exhausted.

Tuesday…

I gotta change my life. I must do something. I must change. It's now or never Sarah.

Wednesday…

Panicky.

Lonely.

Very, very lonely.

A few months later…

Wednesday…

Target reached! Seven stone!

I have so much more confidence!

I am smiling again!

I feel I haven't smiled in years!

My goodness. Do I want to exist again? Like…really exist…be a proper person…?

But it's easier just to hide away in the shadows of life…be a nobody…you don't need to eat…you can live off water…

No! Go away! I am NOT succumbing to your orders anymore! Leave me alone!

I am my own person now. I am proud of who I am.

I do want to exist again.

I am lonely.

I FEEL lonely.

I can feel again!

Congratulations Sarah.

You are on the road to recovery.

The following week…

Monday…

Starting to notice weight gain.

Feel panicky. At home I feel fat. So, so fat. But in my head I know I am ill. I am still anorexic and need food to make me better.

I must keep calm. Calm and collected.

Stick with eating plan. It is working Sarah. Keep up the good work.

Friday...

My stomach hurts so much. I feel so bloated.

Monday...

I am ready.

I am ready to have my life back.

It's a strange feeling.

I feel like I no longer live in the past; like I am slowly edging forwards somehow...

Tuesday...

Utterly exhausted.

Sent a few emails today... walked about aimlessly... crawled back into bed.

Wednesday...

I WANT SO DESPERATELY TO GET BETTER!!!!

Today I believe my ambitions far outweighed reality. I ate too much and too many 'red' foods (see traffic light theory).

I ate cheese, mayonnaise and drank whole milk (which was a big portion of my diet for a couple of years). I continued with crisps, a chocolate bar, a steak, fried mushrooms.....all of which are 'red' foods.

Too many red foods in one day Sarah. Ok, so you want to get better, but just slow down a notch.

Time will heal you; you must be patient.

Thursday...

Last session with Liz. Felt bright and breezy, just like the weather today.

"You've done it Sarah," Liz said to me.

"I couldn't have done it without you...," I said as I gave her a hug, "...you've saved my life Liz."

As she drove off, I felt like I was truly on the road to recovery.

I was overwhelmed with emotion, heartache and desire for life.

To this day I have the upmost appreciation and sincere thanks for all that Liz did and said to me. I will never forget her.

I still remember her gentle tone and patience. Liz's patience was overwhelming.

The following week...

Saturday...

I feel quite normal today. What a bizarre feeling!

Quite balanced and stable!

Nice one!

The next month...

Friday...

Happy.

Several months later...

Friday...

Very focused today at work. Lots of positive energy. I was smiling all day.

Felt like I belong...like I don't want to be invisible anymore.

How very odd.

Saturday...

Very tired.

Lay down on floor.

Monday...

Had drinks last night at party, danced all night long.....hungover today but I don't care!

Feel on top of the world.

My new world.

Wednesday...

Made Christmas table decoration. Being creative brings out the best in me. There are no rights or wrongs.

Thursday....

Tiny, tiny, minute particles far away in another galaxy… she likes it there…

Bitch.

Particles of fine black dust.

You can stay there.

You are a mass of nothingness.

Bitch can stay there and rot.

Rot and die.

You can't get me now.

Following month…

Saturday…

Quite overwhelmed with happiness.

Tuesday…

No need to write in this diary anymore.

It has done its job of getting me better.

Thank you diary.

I will put you in a safe place.

One day I may need you."

E:

Like now!!

S:

"Perhaps one day I will write a book."

E:

Like now!!

S:

"A book about my enthralling life with anorexia and how I became a happy, successful woman.

Yes, I may just do that."

E:

Wowza.

S:

"Cheerio for now little book!"

She Held A Gun To My Head

Part 6

Hospitalisation for Elizabeth

S:

You went into hospital recently for a short time. This was because of my anorexia?

E:

Yes it was, I'm afraid to say.

S:

Really?

E:

Yes. It affected me so much that I could not handle it anymore.

I said to you that I couldn't see you anymore until you sorted yourself out, put weight on and got your life together. This really, really hurt and upset me.

I could barely function.

I found things very difficult.

I remember it was THE single hardest time I have ever, ever cried, in my whole life. I was working only mornings then and in the afternoons I used to listen to

The Fray. I was doing weights one afternoon with The Fray playing, and I remember crying and crying and crying, so hard until I couldn't breathe. I remember looking out the window onto the fields beyond and all I could think about was you.

How strange to have cried like that and never to have told you.

S:

I have apologised this year for how my anorexia has affected you. Well I'll say it again and again, and even in writing...sorry Pea.

E:

As I told you before, I appreciate the apology, I really do, but you don't have to apologise as it wasn't your fault. And I am proud of you for the way you are rejuvenating yourself. You don't need to apologise, but thank you, apology accepted.

I've found an email I wrote to you. I must have written this soon after I told you I couldn't see you until you got yourself pulled together... It goes like this:

"Hiya Sarah,

Re: Where's Sarah?

I realised something last night. The reason I can't see you anymore is that you are not my Sarah anymore. I realised that I've not had my Sarah since school. Seeing the person who is now my twin breaks my heart into a million pieces. Last night I realised I cannot, and will not, lose you as I want my twinny back. I am not prepared to watch you "exist" alone and not reach our 100 years mark together. I'm prepared to help you if you want to make a breakthrough and put this behind you. But I want to stress this: I may as well lose you now if you choose to continue as you are."

So you see, I was preparing to let you go.

"And I know from my own experience [of bulimia] that this is a choice and is only determined by yourself.

A breakthrough means accepting you are a person who has and has had anorexia for fourteen years and changing everything about that person. Fourteen years! A breakthrough will come if you do this – I promise you this one thing – you have to change everything, everything Pea.

You've lost boyfriends, friends, a home, jobs, your dream career [artist], and me for two and a half days. I think/fear you will lose a lot more. In fact I bet you will lose a lot more.

You have two options from me: go further into your anorexia, or file the b****** and start living – with a family and a home of your own.

Don't be afraid to talk to friends and family.

Your twinny,

Billy*

P.S. Pretending (to me) that you have recovered doesn't work - you have to accept what you have to be able to overcome it and move on. Do not fight it. It has nothing to do with me. You have to accept it, otherwise you will live like this until you are old enough to be a grandmother. You still have a girl's body and it's time to have a woman's body. If you do want this Sarah, tell me. As I say, my heart breaks into a million pieces every time I see you."

Since we "made up" after me not wanting to speak to you or see you, I've wanted to write this book. I desperately want to get something good out of your suffering Pea, like being a proud author of a published book. That's why I got a book published about what I went through. It felt so great to get closure from my problems and I do believe you will feel the same way. You will close that part of your life and have the strength to move on to the next chapter. It speeds up the process. I want to help you with the book and be your support, like I was supposed to have been when you had your anorexia. I let you down by saying I couldn't see you anymore, couldn't do it anymore, be the twin to the anorexic; I just couldn't do it. I couldn't bear to see you or even think about you. It tore me up, right to the bone. So much so, I tried to end my own life on two occasions. Cries for help those were, cries for help.

Since we published our magazine article this year, I've realised why I had mental issues and nervous breakdowns, if that's what they were. You see Pea, I felt so guilty that I'd let you down. I said no to you but you didn't know why. I said I didn't want to see you until you were better but you denied you had a problem. Every time I saw you, all I saw was someone else. It wasn't you Pea. It wasn't my Pea. When we were together it wasn't you, I wasn't with you. It was someone else - someone had taken you away from me and I didn't know what to do anymore. I did it for about fourteen years and I couldn't do it anymore, especially once I met my life partner.

I seriously don't know what I'd do if you moved away. SERIOUSLY. I've never actually thought about it until now - how very odd. I don't think I'd like it. This isn't because I wouldn't be able to help you, but because I'd miss you. I want the days of me helping you and you following me over - this wasn't you. You are a DIFFERENT person now; you are Sarah. You help me and support me now. It's different and it's something else being on the same level. It really is something else. I feel like a proper twin now. What a strange thing to say. You are still my little twin sister, but you are stronger now, you are Sarah, your own person. THIS is why I had to let you go when you were anorexic - you were nobody to me. Sarah had gone. You even said you had died in your body. I felt this too and because of this, I wanted to take my own life. I wanted to cross over to the spirit world so I felt no more guilt, no more pain. I didn't want Mam and Dad to be disappointed in me as I couldn't help you, I couldn't do this to them. So I thought it would be easier not to deal with them and just leave for another world. A world where I thought there would be no pain. I got so involved in this that I could think of nothing else. I even saw the entrance to the spirit world and looked into it. I saw the painless world and thought of it day and night. I was losing touch with reality and perhaps the only thing that kicked me into action was wanting to be with my life partner. Together we got help and I went into hospital, where I was observed 24 hours a day. You and I weren't speaking at this point so you didn't come to the hospital. I was in there for eight days. Those eight days changed my life, and yours too I think.

S:

What things about my anorexia affected you?

E:

The fact that I couldn't have a life. You were so dependent on me. Your whole life was shaped around food and the fact that you had to control it, so you didn't really have the strength to think about anything else. You couldn't keep a job, stay at one place for long or have a relationship of your own. This was difficult for me. I loved it when you came to visit me – at university in Bristol, in The Netherlands, even in New York - but I felt you were following me. I wanted to be with you but not to the extent where we couldn't have our own lives. This was so important to me – for us to be our own people.

S:

I wasn't following you; it was because I didn't have my own life. I didn't have the strength to have my own life.

E:

Yes, I appreciate that.

There were also little signs of your anorexia that I couldn't live with anymore, especially when I moved into your little flat with you. The doctor put you on some tablets that made you tired in the evening. In fact you were so tired that you wouldn't even respond to me. I felt like you hated me. Then you used to spend ages deciding what to have for sweet after dinner.

We had problems with our stomachs because of our anxiety, and we were recommended the York Test. We took this and we stuck by the results – we were intolerant to bread and milk so we stopped eating them, and your cupboard in your flat got full of expensive free-from food goods. You became obsessed and so did I.

My anxiety got worse when I lived with you in that flat. I would spend up to an hour deciding what to wear to go out, even to visit family just around the corner. I would stand in front of my wardrobe, try everything on, panic would set in and you would get annoyed. Eventually you would leave without me and I would arrive later, quite upset. I was in a state then, a right state. I thought I was pathetic. I had no control over myself.

There were other little things that you used to do that affected me. When you ate an apple you would set it down on your lap, let go of it, chew and chew and look around, then pick it up again. It would take you ages as you went through these stages. You would do the same with magazines - you'd read it, then put it down and look about. I think this is all about having control of a situation. It would grind on me and I hated being in the same room.

But you did do some things that made me proud of you and this was while you had the anorexia. I was so proud when you had your art studio and business. I was proud to be your twin then. You had done this on your own and you even had your name above the door! I used to come and visit your studio – I loved it in there. I would look around all the nooks and crannies, and look with interest at your new work. I loved your art, every little bit. You put so much into it. You'd draw when we were away - in New York, Amsterdam. You even drew when you went to Kilimanjaro. There's something else I am so proud of you for doing! Trying to climb that mountain, with a petite body like yours! I was worried and so pleased you came back in one piece.

Part 7

Sarah's Wake-Up Call and Therapy

E:

You say you had a wake-up call. What happened?

S:

On the 25th of March 2008 I realised I was suffering from anorexia, and it hit me like a ton of bricks. I cried for a week. I didn't know what to do or where to put myself. I signed myself off sick; for how long I'd be off I didn't know. I didn't know how long it would take me to get better or how could I ever make up for the fourteen years I had lost. I now sincerely believe I have lost fourteen years of my life.

E:

Let's talk about your therapy. What did it include?

S:

Well I've brought along my folders, which I've not opened since the therapy. I have two folders, from two therapies:

- Eating specialist

- Cognitive behavioural therapy to manage my OCD (off set from anorexia)

Any time I wrote anything, my therapist told me to highlight certain words.

I am quite excited to look through these folders!

E:

Why?

S:

Because it's just, err (scratches head)...it just seems to be funny.

E:

Funny haha?

S:

I don't know. I think not funny haha. I can't believe I went through all this. Looking at it feels a bit pathetic. Such time wasted, but I was ill and it had to be done.

E:

It's weird because it's not like a course for a job, or a qualification. You've done it in your spare time and got no qualifications. It's weird.

S:

Yes I totally agree. Now, with a healthy mind, I can see it from an outsider's point of view - this therapy was highly necessary for me, but only when I had accepted that I had anorexia.

When I was in therapy, I was asked to do homework. I had to write a compassionate letter to myself, from myself. It goes like this:

Dear Sarah,

Hello. I understand that you have been through quite a lot over the past ten years or so. From what I hear you have been quite ill. But fortunately you have a strong personality and your own self belief has pulled you through. People like you are fighters. You could have taken the easiest route, but you are strong and are still here.

Anorexia is an illness, just like when you break a leg or get gum disease. It's something that happens to the body which can happen to anyone. It's no-one's fault. It's life. We all must deal with what life gives us, even if it is hard.

Even during the time of your illness when you were at your weakest and the anorexia had completely taken over you, you were still able to do things that were so positive. Sarah, you climbed a mountain! You raised £3,000 for vulnerable children! You even had a couple of boyfriends!

It is not your fault that you have had anorexia; you must not blame yourself. There are so many other boys and girls in the world that have been and are going through the same thing. I MUST REPEAT – it is an illness. Just like if you have angina or need an operation. It is a medical illness - mental or physical, it doesn't matter which - and the individual is not to blame.

You must treat the illness with respect - treat it with care and consideration. If you broke your arm, you wouldn't start to do press ups, would you? So treat your anorexia with respect. You must give it time to heal. Don't rush it.

Life isn't fair, we all know that. The nicest, most loving people get ill, through no fault of their own. It's part of life. It's part of being born, living and dying. And I know you're not scared of dying."

This is so serious and boring, I'm depressing myself...

E:

But...?

S:

It is highly relevant and was crucial for my therapy.

Anyway...to continue...

"You overcame your fear of death when you developed anorexia. When you realised that life is just part of the universe, and we are all just little dots. Without death, the universe couldn't evolve and time would become still. But time is moving, evolution is evolving, and we are like little beings that live and die within this process.

You should not punish yourself either. IT IS NOT YOUR FAULT. I must keep repeating myself until you realise this. I know it's going to take time Sarah, but you know that cancer patients shouldn't punish themselves, so you should not either.

You deserve to be happy, just like everybody else - just like the person walking down the street or the person sitting on the coffee shop.

You were so happy as a child. You were so popular at school. You were so happy when you were camping in France and swimming in the sea. You didn't think about anything apart from how happy you were, and how life was so easy and nice. It is now Sarah, you have just forgotten about all the good things. You loved having your photograph taken, chatting with others, meeting new people, being involved in everything; doing things - dancing, laughing, watching telly, learning. You were never cold; you never had bad thoughts. You were always smiling.

So be that girl again Sarah. Let's say you've had time out in life. Maybe you needed this time - it was just life's way of telling you to take a step back.

No more thinking about what you have or haven't done. Life isn't about the past, it's about the here and now, and things to look forward to.

You've been through so much, you should be proud of yourself that you've survived. Think of it as a life test which you passed. A few times you nearly gave up but because you're a fighter, you made it over the finish line. You won.

So you can move on now, you are done with that."

E:

Can you buy a t-shirt?

S:

Don't be stupid! Talk about labelling!

"Well done! You've been to hell and back - no wonder you are exhausted. It's time to have fun again! Become that Sarah you have longed to be, not the anorexic Sarah who was ready to die. No wonder you felt so old. You were ready to give up, you thought it was your time.

Show some compassion for yourself Sarah. Stop beating yourself up, you don't deserve it. You deserve to be happy and free.

Hope you get well very soon - I'm sure you will. I have every faith in you, as I am sure you do too.

Kindest Regards

Sarah"

She Held A Gun To My Head

Part 8

Managing the Anorexia

E:

I've only started calling you Pea because I only thought you were my Pea after you admitted you had anorexia. Before this, I had no Pea. It was a selfish thing inside you that dictated you and hid the real Sarah for many years.

So what things do you have to deal with as a result of the anorexia?

S:

As a recovering anorexic, I deal with things in my head. One of these things is OCD – Obsessive Compulsive Disorder. It developed towards the end of my anorexia and takes up a big part of my life.

E:

Hmmm.

S:

I have thought of a little advert:

An apple a day may kill you (if you're anorexic)

Monday	Apple
Tuesday	Apple
Wednesday	Apple
Thursday	Apple
Friday	Apple
Saturday	Apple
Sunday	Apple

E:

This poem is really good! I always did relate you with eating apples all the time.

So would you say you manage your anorexia?

S:

Yes. I manage it. I have good weeks and bad weeks. And compared to what I used to be like, I definitely manage it. I am currently receiving cognitive behavioural therapy for my OCD and am slowly overcoming my demons.

E:

I see.

S:

I have things that keep me going, such as my life management plan/structure - I LOVE bullet points, goals - annual, monthly, weekly, daily and even hourly. Plans too! I love to plan, but I am also very, very spontaneous. You say I was even like this before I had anorexia in my teens, always doing something wild that would make you cringe!

What really got me through was my inner strength, something inside me. This is why I don't regret having it - I now feel that I have an iron core. Nothing now will upset, stop or hinder me from doing the things I want to do.

Often memories come flooding back and I'm overwhelmed with emotion. Sadness, not for myself because I know how happy I am now, but for other anorexics and their families. Also happiness – words can't describe how happy I am to be alive. I'm so happy to be alive! And nothing will take this feeling away. I have an immense appreciation for life.

E:

You even did a skydive and weren't even scared, you nutter. I did one and was SO scared!

S:

I know! I would do it again and again and again!

I used to draw figures, always figures of the body. I had about ten sketch books which I threw away into a skip I found somewhere, I can't even remember where. All I remember is that they were in a bin bag and I drove somewhere. I was in a panic. The sketch books had drawings of figures, slashy, quick drawings. I just wanted to get rid of the books. Now that I think about it, it didn't feel like me drawing. It felt like the anorexia was drawing through me.

E:

Okay, I'd like to ask you some questions I've never asked you before.

Do you regret having anorexia?

S:

No.

E:

How do you feel when you say the word "anorexia"?

S:

Give me a few moments to have a think...

...I am gutted that it got me. I could have been something much more than what I am. And I feel like it has taken my life...

...I feel crushed for myself and for other sufferers.

E:

How do you feel when you see other anorexics, say, in the street or on the television?

S:

Gutted for them. I want to help them. I don't want to go and give them a shake; perhaps I don't want to talk to them directly. I just want them to find the strength I did, to fight it. And when I see anorexics who are older than me, or have had it for years, it absolutely crushes me.

E:

How do you feel now, since admitting you have had anorexia, towards your friends, family, and towards yourself?

S:

Elated, liberated...

...I am no longer embarrassed and I feel proud of who I am now.

E:

How has your confidence and self-esteem been since admitting you have had anorexia?

S:

It's increased slowly, as my mind is still getting used to it - re-jiggling all the thoughts has been a shock. But now, with acceptance, my confidence has shot through the roof and now there's no going back. Often I sit on my own and realise how lucky I am.

E:

How did you feel when you had anorexia?

S:

Dead. Is that a good enough answer? I was no good to anybody.

E:

What is the one tip that you would give to close friends and family of those who are suffering from anorexia?

S:

Oh dear this is a hard question! Something has to click in their head for them to get better.

E:

Did you ever stop and wonder how I felt when you had anorexia?

S:

No, I could not feel.

E:

What went through your mind when I told you I didn't want to see you unless you helped yourself and put weight on?

S:

Shit.

E:

What five things would you advise to anorexia sufferers?

S:

Five things?

1. Don't be alone;
2. Team work;
3. Share;
4. Write;
5. Be inspired.

E:

What would you like to say to Mam and Dad, now you've admitted having anorexia?

S:

Hiya! You don't have to worry about me anymore because I am managing it now, like Elizabeth manages her mental health.

E:

Are you proud of yourself now you've stepped up and admitted to yourself, and to the world, that you have had anorexia and are now trying to get better?

S:

Hell yeah.

E:

Do you think the fully fledged anorexia can return, or do you think it can be fought off forever?

S:

I don't know.

E:

Do you think about your past life now?

S:

Yes and I feel joyful and lucky to have survived because I did think I was going to die.

E:

What was the worst thing about your anorexia?

S:

The pain.

E:

What is your worst memory of your anorexia?

S:

The pain, the cold, everything felt HARD. I remember it was painful just lying in bed. That's why I could never sit still anywhere.

E:

Are you proud of yourself for having lived through anorexia and having beaten it? Could you become an ambassador and help others like you were?

S:

Definitely, yes.

E:

What would you do if you met an anorexic the same age as you? What would you say to them? Would you want to hide away, or would you want to try to help and offer kind words?

S:

Help.

E:

So, even though you have these things like OCD still to deal with, would you firmly say that you are rebuilding your life?

S:

Yes. As I keep saying to you, I feel I have lost fourteen years, and I've got all this to catch up on. My aim is to rebuild my life, definitely.

E:

And you think you're on the right track?

S:

Oh yes!

I want to give some solid advice in the form of strategies which I used during therapy, but which I will continue to use throughout my life.

Number 1: Face a fear – Put yourself in an uncomfortable situation on a daily basis. Fear meaning scared, frightened, nervous, embarrassed...

E:

You mean like a job interview?

S:

Yes, or a date! Anything that gets you out of your comfort zone.

Number 2: Break the routine – It is good to have a routine but be flexible about it. Do something spontaneous. Or watch a late night movie.

Number 3: Do something for someone – Make a birthday card, give a massage, wash someone's car, talk to a friend.

Number 4: Learn something new – Erm...Read up on the Prime Minister.

E:

I know...do a crossword.

S:

Pick up the dictionary and learn a new word.

Number 5: Be creative – make something, anything. Just use your hands, even if it is naff.

Number 6 : Plan something – A girls' night out, a day out shopping with your mam, a coffee with your friend...

Number 7: Keep a positive diary

E:

My therapist advised me to make a happy box to put all my happy things in. So I bought a wooden box and put in all my old stuff, like birthday cards!

S:

...Every night, write five positive things that you appreciated that day.

Number 8: Surround yourself with positivity – People, colour, crystals and happiness!

E:

What always made me happy was going to a town, sitting in a coffee shop with a newspaper and people-watching.

S:

...Or you could watch a comedy, wear yellow, meditate and do yoga - even better, do it outside!

Number 9: Wear different colours – Yellow! Pink, orange, peach, green, white. There are lots of colours we can all wear and I do believe they affect our mood.

Number 10: Phone a friend

Number 11: Take a dog for a walk

Number 12: Set short term (daily) goals – Drink water, learn three new words, go and chat to someone you don't know.

There's something that's stuck out in my mind...wait till I find it...here it is...

'The Mechanics of Weight Gain' (Gilbert, S., *Counselling for Eating Disorders*, Sage Publications, 2000).

Before I read this, I thought that I just had to eat a bit more to put weight on and be normal again. However, upon reading this (over and over and over again to make myself believe it), I learnt that as an anorexic I had to eat several horses a day.

E:

Huh?

S:

I had to eat up to 3000 calories a day in order to become a healthy weight, but I'd have to be eating this amount for several months before any weight appeared. This is because my vital organs had been starved and needed feeding first. So the first few months of eating normal food was an absolute nightmare.

E:

I seem to remember you tried this on a few occasions before, but then you stopped and returned back to "anorexic" eating, because the amount of food you had to consume was simply too much.

S:

Yes. But this time I had accepted I had anorexia and something had clicked in my mind. Therefore I was willing to eat as much as I had to, even if I felt like absolute crap. I was so tired!

E:

Who told you to eat this way?

S:

My Eating Disorder specialist.

E:

I see, that's good.

S:

Yes, you could say she saved my life.

E:

So...

S:

I just want us to get on with our lives, get this book published and move forward now.

E:

Great.

Interview Ends.

She Held A Gun To My Head

Poems written by Sarah

<u>Traffic Light</u>

How amazing to breathe again

To fill my lungs with life and energy

To fuel my body with love and laughter

I don't remember laughing when anorexia was with me

Laughing was forbidden

Smiling was not allowed

To smile was to let go, to enjoy oneself

Under the wing of anorexia I had strict instructions that I had to follow

Each day when I woke, the rules and regulations were set out for the day ahead

I lay quietly in bed, while 'it' told me the day's agenda

What to eat, what not to eat

What exercise to do

And the timing was crucial

To eat within the hour three times a day, no snacking allowed

To drink only water, either lukewarm or hot (my body systems could not withstand cold temperatures)

Black coffee, no milk

Sugar

Sugar for energy

A little carbs for exercising

A little protein for muscle strength

Greens, lots and lots of greens

There were safe foods

And there were danger foods

Like a traffic light

Green for go, all safe

Red for stop, danger

There were foods in the middle too, foods that I could eat and feel slight anxiety, but still manage to hold it together

Apples were my safety net

I could eat apples forever, Braeburn, Cox, granny smith, red delicious, golden delicious, McIntosh

In a way apples made me feel like I had eaten a lot, due to their crunchiness

Yet within a short while of munching an apple, I was still hungry

So having eaten and to still feel hungry was great

I wasn't disobeying the rules of anorexia

To have eaten and to be satisfiably full would be a sin

Apples, coffee, brown rice, broccoli, carrots, all green foods

Notice coffee is in the safe food list

Everything that passed my lips was classed as a food

Water was a necessity

I would drink water until I felt so bloated and full that my stomach couldn't take anymore

So I had made myself full with water, fooling my stomach that it was full, so didn't have to eat any food

I had obeyed the rules of anorexia

Crisps, chocolate, mayonnaise, white bread, sandwiches bought from the shop,

Pizza, cake, nice yoghurts, nuts, cereals, cheese,

All banned

Sharing food, a big no no

Red foods represented danger

Red foods brought guilt, anger, resentment, hatred, and most of all punishment

To eat a red food I had to punish myself

Starve myself for hours, go on a long run, two to three hours, use up all the energy I had put into my body

Get rid of all the toxins I had sinfully given in to

Toxins that were bad, nasty and unnecessary

Chewing gum was banned

Chewing gum was unnecessary food that would contain some fat

So my favourite gums were forbidden

When a friend asked if I wanted a piece of their gum, I would decline immediately and become offensive

But deep inside I so longed to share their 'treat' and be a part of the real world

A sweet would upset me, set me off track

A Greggs sandwich would make me feel so guilty, so angry and disgusted with myself

A bar of chocolate would have me in turmoil for days

Everything had been ruined, giving in to a red food

I had to punish myself for days after, get rid of all the toxins and start again

It was a vicious circle

A circle I couldn't get out of

Round and round, starting fresh then having something that wasn't 'correct'

So I would have to start all over again, starving myself and making sure my body was empty

Round and round until my head hurt so much

All the thoughts were concentrated in this circle

Nothing else mattered

I was exhausted to the world

A surreal, loveless, sinful world of emptiness, starvation and punishment

Red, amber, green

The bright colours of the traffic light

Stop, get ready, go

Die, eat, live

Anorexia was my traffic light

The control system in my head

I no longer had a normal functioning brain, it had been seduced by this 'thing'

I had the mental capacity of a corpse

Anorexia had come into my brain and taken over, it was my government

To live by the rules of anorexia were to live properly and correctly

To be safe and secure

If I reached its daily goals and targets I would be rewarded

Rewarded with the satisfaction of immense achievement

Achievement that I had reached, all by myself

I didn't need anyone or anything else

I didn't need food

The only thing I needed was my control system keeping me right, keeping me on the right track

My anorexia was my world

When it was in me I loved it, the feeling of achievement and satisfaction was overwhelming

That was my fuel, my energy, the self achievement it gave me

The knowing that I had reached my goals without the need of anything or anyone

Anorexia made me believe I could live with nothing

No love, no feelings, no emotions, no relationships, no food, no treats, no happiness

What a joke that was

A dark black evil joke that I can only hearing anorexia laughing to

She was my Best Friend

I am so sorry for what I have done

For the pain I have caused

The hurt, the anger, the sorrow

The sadness is overwhelming

The sadness I have caused for fourteen years

Yet it wasn't me who caused the pain

I swear it wasn't me

Anorexia did it, she did it all

I do not blame myself

I cannot blame myself, for she is the guilty one

She held the gun to my head

For I know now what anorexia is, what she can do

She was my control panel, my brain, my lungs, my heart

She kept me alive, without her I would have been nothing

But I understand now what she did

It is so sad what she did to me

She was deep inside me, I could feel her touching my heart

My soul, I felt her breathing in me, breathing for me

She controlled my every breath

She was my best friend

She told me how to live, how to behave and how to control

She taught me how to starve

She said it was good to starve

To starve was to feel nice, to starve was to feel

To starve was to feel alive

She loved me and I adored her

I worshipped her, she made me feel alive

I felt alive, yet my body was starving, my mind exhausted

So alive that I could do anything, I felt I was flying through air, through space

No one could touch me, no one could get close

She was my protection against the world

With her inside me, no-one could hurt me

No-one could ever hurt me

She made me happy, she was all I needed

She was my friend for a long time

She taught me to live, how to behave, what to wear and what to eat

More importantly what not to eat

The less I ate the more alive I felt, no-one could touch me

No one could hurt me, I was flying

Flying for fourteen years

The Pain

The worst was the pain, the bitterly cold pain that would never go away

The second I opened my eyes in the morning, the pain would hit me like a smack in the face

My legs hurt so much, my stomach screamed for nourishment

My fingertips were freezing, I couldn't bear to touch my own skin

They were so cold

The holistic pain was often unbearable, my whole body aching

I could feel the pounding of my heart as it tried so hard to get blood around my body

I thought it was going to explode, it was working so hard

Yet the pain didn't register, the anorexia too powerful

I denied my own body what it ached for

I carried on floating in pain, consuming as little as I dared possible

I knew something wasn't right, I never felt like this as a child

I always remember having such a happy childhood

So what had gone wrong, why did I feel so much pain?

I often thought if everyone else felt like this, felt the excruciating pain I could feel...

But they were always smiling, laughing, making jokes

I didn't understand what was so funny

What were they all laughing at

They were laughing and I was screaming

Screaming so hard inside that it hurt

But no-one could hear me

I knew they couldn't hear me

Anorexia knew they couldn't hear me

It had shut me off from them, from my friends, my family, my world

Anorexia had cost me everything, my world, my life, my love, my touch

Anorexia had the power to do that

It had become my world

The world without life, love, touch

The only feeling it let me have was pain

And I thrived off it

The pain kept me going, it kept me feeling alive

Without the pain I would have not felt, I believe I may have died

The power of anorexia is so strong that it can kill

Anorexia can kill and does kill

It goes beyond pain, it strives and reaches high enough until it can reach no further

Pain becomes unbearable until death is the only option left

But something inside me was strong enough for 'it' not to kill me

I stood up to 'its' power and fought

I was strong enough to do that

I didn't let the pain kill me

I wouldn't let the pain kill me

I could live with the pain for as long as anorexia had its control

But I could not live with anorexia winning

Not a chance in hell

The Cold

I remember the only feeling I had was the cold

I didn't just feel the cold, I was the cold

My skin, numb to the elements, so cold and bitter

My face was blue, there was no colour left, no colour of happiness or inner joy

No exercise could warm my blood

The faster and harder I ran, the colder I became

200 sit-ups, 50 press-ups, there was no heat

I had no energy to create heat

It's not rocket science

Energy creates heat

But anorexia diminishes all reasoning

My mind had lost all logic and rationale

I know the body needs energy to exercise, to move

I'm not stupid

Yet with anorexia my mind was blind to reality

I had to eat less, to exercise more, just to gain success and achievement

So my body was cold

My bones were cold

When I lay in bed, even in pyjamas under a thick duvet and blanket, I was cold

My bones hurt in bed

My bones hurt especially in the bath

Yet that was the only place I felt a little warmth

I would sit in the bath until my core temperature was hot

But minutes after leaving the bath I would be cold once again

The joy of being anorexic

Here are some scribbles I wrote in my journal:

Sarah wasn't real.

I was a walking skeleton.

When I exercise I do every movement as well as I can. I must concentrate on pushing myself.

When you're unhappy with the way you look and feel, it doesn't matter where you go or what you do…you'll be forever unhappy.

Depression is a symptom of dying, for which living is the cure.

We are most alive when we are laughing.

I want to fly away, fly away with all my might, fly away, above the dogs, the dirt, I want to fly with no-one, fly with all the evil inside me, the evil I despise.

I want to be the music inside me, feel it come out, I need it outside me. I want to compose, eat , sleep, shower, here, now. I want to compose but I can't. I don't feel anything, I can't hear anything, where is it?

I am in a meadow, no-one else is here. I don't know why, perhaps they don't like it. I can hear the music now, it's amazing, it's beautiful. Why won't they come dance with me?

It's a beautiful evening, I am sat on a boathouse watching the water. I am not speaking tonight. I have no mouth. I am so tired.

Slowly waking up to my Demon

I've had it, I am so tired. I can barely speak. I've had enough.

Sad, pathetic memories. Anorexia has stretched me as far as I can go.

I need dancing, colours, to be wild!

Pathetic obsession with food.

What's the point?

It doesn't make you happy.

Get a grip you stupid stupid bitch!

I know to eat three meals a day.

I know a yellow room is a happy space.

I know the body needs protein for strength and carbohydrates for energy.

But tell that to my anorexia. She doesn't care what's good for you.

She is evil. She enjoys watching you starve, watching you waste into nothing.

An empty body, one that was so happy, so full of life and sunshine.

Anyway, she's not even listening. She doesn't give a damn.

She tells me not to listen and I do as I am told.

Goddamn it, I wish
I hadn't listened.

The stupid bitch.

The stupid evil bitch.

How fantastic to breathe again

I am so angry

Angry at myself

Angry at falling beneath its power

Its power was so strong, I couldn't let go

It held me captive for fourteen years

It starved me

It made me so hungry I could no longer see

It blinded me from the world, from myself

I would look in the mirror and see an alien

Something that didn't exist here

Something that was void of emotion

Void of feeling, breath and future

This something that stared back at me was horrible

Disgusting

I hated what I saw

I hated that I couldn't feel, I couldn't touch, I could barely see

This thing that stared back at me

I wanted it dead

Dead

It was like a living corpse, with sunken eyes

Staring at me

What the hell was it looking at

I wanted it dead

Stop staring at me you freak

Stop looking at me, I will kill you

If you don't take your black eyes off me I will kill you

Stab you right through your heart

That'll stop you punishing me

You always punish me

Punish me for trying to live

Punish me for trying to love

Without you I could breathe again

I could love again

Please stop looking

Turn your head away and let me go

Let me breathe again

Let me love again

I need to breathe

Please

I'm not ready to die yet

Let me go

She betrayed me

Now I understand that she was my anorexia

My anorexia lived with me for fourteen long years

A life time

Wasted

I can see now from the outside that I wasn't flying, I was floating

Floating through each day like a corpse

I was a person living inside a dead being

My body was so starved it couldn't possibly function

I could barely move

I remember vividly how hard it was to breathe

Each breath was so shallow, so long and deep that often I felt I would stop breathing

I visited the doctor on numerous occasions, demanding tests on my heart

I was adamant my heart was failing and I was going to die

My anorexia hadn't surfaced yet and I really believed I had heart failure

I was in denial for so long

Anorexia had set in and my mind had been taken over by this evil, evil thing

A thing I imagined (and still do, the image will never leave me) as a green, malicious creature

A creature I have never seen before

Yet I knew it so well

It felt like it belonged in me, and at the time it felt warm, safe, secure

I didn't ever want to let it go

But this creature inside me, I suddenly realized it was going to kill me

I was going to die

I was 29 and if I didn't release this creature, I wasn't going to see my 30th birthday

One morning I woke up and I was so overwhelmed with anxiety, depression, panic, suffering, heartache that I thought I was going to have a heart attack

I thought this was my time

I truly believed I was dying

In a strange, bizarre way which I could never explain

My mind was so tangled up, so out of focus, that I thought I would reach for a knife and stab myself right through the heart

A thought I have had for many years, something I have never told anyone

But my heart was calling out

It was crying for help

For me to stop and breathe again

At this point the anorexia seemed to leave my head, go upwards and fade into nothing

It was utterly surreal, like something in another world

But it felt so real, like it was meant to be

I was flooded with emotions and I ran for help

I cried and ran for the help I had been longing for for so many years

I declared myself sick

Sick with the evilness of anorexia

I was so drowned with sorrow, hurt, anger and hatred that my body became numb to the outside world

I could barely speak

I remember crying for a full week

I hugged myself and wouldn't let go

Anorexia had nearly killed me

It had come so close

But something inside me had woken up, it had seen that death was so close

That was the Sarah inside me

The Sarah who wanted to live

To see the sunshine again and to feel the grass beneath her feet

She wanted to feel the air on her face, the freezing cold air hitting her so hard that it hurt

She wanted to feel the love, the pain, the compassion of other human beings

She wanted to feel loved, be loved and to love

She wanted to be touched, to touch and to feel her body again

Unnecessary evils of OCD

Why think about unnecessary evils which may never come

Evils that don't exist, evils that don't belong

Think about the existence you're in

Listen, look, feel

Feel the air against your face

Feel the sounds

See the sounds floating in the air

There are no evils here

Evils live in the darkness

The darkness which you can't see

Stop punishing yourself for something that doesn't exist

OCD lives in the darkness

The air is fresh where everyone else is, the place where you should be

It is so dark down there

No one can hear you when you go down there

It is so clear and pure up here

Simple

There are no numbers here, you can stop counting

Counting won't bring love, counting to four won't make everything ok

One, two, three, four

One, two, three, four

Sets of one, two, three, ten

Sometimes even thirty

Over and over and over again

Counting sets until the numbers are no longer numbers

They don't make sense

My vision is blurred and I feel faint

The world is no longer real

I can't breathe

I can't see

Panic, numbers, dizzy, faint, must finish off the sets

Can't think until I finish off counting

The world has gone

I can't hear people talking to me

My breathing stops

And then I can see again

I realize I am not breathing and gasp for air

I resist punching myself and scratching my skin

What the hell just happened here

I take a few deep breaths and hold my head up high

I shake my head and think of all the positives in life

Why does this happen over and over and over

Sometimes all the time, in my head, even when I am lying in bed

Even when I am not doing anything, I am still checking and counting

Even when I turn the light off and wish it all to go away

Shut everything off so my mind is free to rest

Yet the counting is still there, the breathing still stops and starts

Welcome to my world of OCD

Pea

Billy billy pea pea pea

Oh shiny happy smiling pea.

Shining always, even when low.

Always bright, colourful and neat.

Thinking and zoning her life, like it was the only one she's got.

Zoning and packing only good times into her days.

Her life shining onto everyone around her.

Bringing people close to her like she was a strong magnet.

Electro-pulses leaving her every breath.

Reflecting and bouncing optimism off every corner she sees.

Touching the hearts of everyone she hears.

Spying and discovering new feelings every day.

Pea brings sunshine into a room on entrance.

Pea reflects happiness from her everyday doings and rituals.

Pea follows love and peace from the magic that flows deep within the Earth's heart.

Pea bounces off every corner of everyday drudgery and comes up a shining light from the darkest of holes.

Pea's peace with herself and the world is all so strong and dominant.

It often hurts and fills people with envy and jealousy.

Her peace and silence, coming from deep within, reflects her uppermost self, being and character.

Only her feelings and emotions can be found deep within her heart and soul.

Pea must keep with all her heart touching rituals and zones in order to survive the world around her.

Sunshine only comes from a few hearts and must not be sustained from freedom, restrained from those willing to give, or kept hidden beneath the greyest of clouds.

Even in the darkest, quietest places of the world, Pea touches the hearts of every grain of sand that flows in the breeze of the wind.

She must not be kept hidden from deep, hurtful feelings that often begrudge those who let it behold them.

Pea is strong and can hold the strongest of winds high above the oceans on the planets.

Pea is full of peace, laughter and sunshine and no heart-filled love, rose-scented pillow or champagne-filled glass will ever fulfil my needs like Pea does.

Pea x

Being a Twin

Being a twin is the most amazing thing

To be loved so unconditionally

To have been so close to another human being

To have lived and loved apart, yet still so close

I close my eyes and we are still as one

One human being as two, living and loving separate lives

Still fusing as one, yet running as two

The most amazing feeling in the world

Yet to be as one separate being I would not know

As my existence with my soulmate is all I know

Being a twin is a funny thing

A lovely, wonderful, beautiful thing

I sometimes cry when I think of losing her

If she left I would follow

For living without her would be so dark

I would follow with her into the sunlight

The sun always shines when I think of her

Being a twin is the most beautiful thing in the world

Beautiful sunshine on a bright, breezy day

Unconditional love is there always

We know what the other is thinking, feeling and knowing

We look at one another and we need not speak

For we understand and feel the same

Often we need not look or talk

I understand her and she understands me

I find it difficult to describe in words

If you were my twin, you'd understand

Not with Roses

Not with roses

Not with scent

Or star filled dreams

But with hands

Heart and breath

Here

In this surreal reality

I say

I love you Pea.

Poem written by Elizabeth

A Little Pea Kiss

We were young twins and we competed for status,

Setting high standards and not knowing how dangerous.

You were popular and I was shy,

We went off to uni, so far away, but why?

We started to have problems in our late teens,

We did not know but this was not in our genes.

Brought on ourselves for wanting to be heard,

Not once did we speak about it, not a word.

I went afar, and tried to make myself my own,

But I always knew you were there, staying close to home.

Every time I saw you my heart broke and crumbled,

For I knew you were sad, and lonely, and jumbled.

You were poorly, couldn't settle, and losing weight,

The more I saw you, my life I began to hate.

The guilt, the frustration, and the guilt once more,

Started to eat me up, really down to the core.

You were my twin, my sister, the closest friend I had,

I ended up saying go away, go away, and for this I was not glad.

I was a mess and you were too,

We didn't speak for a while, not even to say boo.

I was in hospital, and I realised I had to stop feeling responsible,

For it was your life, and for me to help you was just not possible.

I envisioned myself getting more and more blue,

Months and months did pass, I really had no clue.

Now the time has come, you have sought help, just like me,

Every time I see you, you are better and better, that's my beautiful Pea.

All I ever wanted was for us to be happy,

To see each other often, to be wild and wacky.

I once felt extremely trapped and responsible being the elder twin,

So much so I wanted to put myself in the bin.

All I want to do now is tell you I'm sorry,

Because I couldn't look after you, sorry, sorry, sorry.

There's just one more thing, I wish you all the best Pea.

Thank you so, so much for looking after me, and understanding me.

You are one in a million, did anyone ever tell you this?

You are very special too, goodnight, sweet dreams, and a little pea kiss (or high five, whichever you prefer).

She Held A Gun To My Head

www.ingramcontent.com/pod-product-compliance
Lightning Source LLC
Chambersburg PA
CBHW031210270326
41931CB00006B/498